The
BOOZY BARD

Shakespeare on Drinking

CHARTWELL
BOOKS, INC.

This edition published in 2006 by
CHARTWELL BOOKS, INC.
A division of BOOK SALES, INC.
114 Northfield Avenue
Edison, New Jersey 08837
USA

ISBN-13: 978-0-7858-2131-1
ISBN-10: 0-7858-2131-7

Summersdale Publishers Ltd
46 West Street
Chichester
West Sussex
PO19 1RP
UK

Printed and bound in Spain

Contents

Introduction

Mary and John Shakespeare's eldest son William was born in April 1564, in the Warwickshire town of Stratford-Upon-Avon. Before William was born, the couple had two daughters, but in an age haunted by the Plague, both girls died while still babies. Thankfully for us William survived this terrible sixteenth century disease, and created a huge body of work that became the most notable milestone in English literature – yet enjoyed life to the full and sadly drank himself to death in his early fifties. The Vicar of Stratford put it thus: 'Shakespeare, Drayton, and Ben Jonson had a merry meeting and it seems drank too hard, for Shakespeare died of a fever there contracted.'

We thought it only right to salute our beer-loving ancestor with this tasteful selection of quips and observations. The Bard had so much to say about drink, drinking and drinkers that we've categorised it all by play (or poem). Whatever your favourite Shakespeare classic – be it *Romeo and Juliet*, *Macbeth* or *King Lear* – you'll find its boozy gems in here.

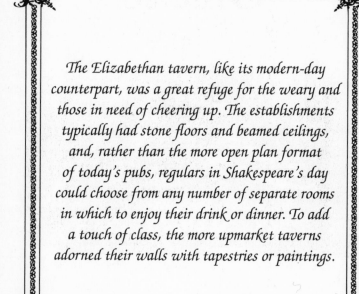

The Elizabethan tavern, like its modern-day counterpart, was a great refuge for the weary and those in need of cheering up. The establishments typically had stone floors and beamed ceilings, and, rather than the more open plan format of today's pubs, regulars in Shakespeare's day could choose from any number of separate rooms in which to enjoy their drink or dinner. To add a touch of class, the more upmarket taverns adorned their walls with tapestries or paintings.

Othello

IAGO

Blessed fig's-end! **the wine she drinks is made of grapes**: if she had been blessed, she would never have loved the Moor.

Act 2, Scene 1

IAGO

Well, happiness to their sheets! Come, lieutenant, I have **a stoup of wine**; and here without are a brace of Cyprus gallants that would fain have a **measure** to the health of black Othello.

CASSIO

Not to-night, good Iago: I have very poor and **unhappy brains for drinking**: I could well wish courtesy would invent some other custom of entertainment.

IAGO

O, they are our friends; but one cup: I'll drink for you.

CASSIO

I have **drunk but one cup** to-night, and that was
craftily qualified too, and, behold, what innovation
it makes here: I am unfortunate in the infirmity,
and dare not task my weakness with any more.

IAGO

What, man! 'tis a night of revels: the gallants
desire it.

IAGO

If I can fasten but one cup upon him,
With that which he hath **drunk** to-night already,
He'll be as full of quarrel and offence
As my young mistress' dog.

The Boozy Bard

CASSIO

'Fore God, they have given me a rouse already.

MONTANO

Good faith, a little one; **not past a pint**, as I am
a soldier.

IAGO

Some wine, ho!
[Sings] And let me the canakin clink, clink;
And let me the canakin clink
A soldier's a man;
A life's but a span;
Why, then, **let a soldier drink**.
Some wine, boys!

CASSIO

'Fore God, an excellent song.

IAGO

I learned it in England, where, indeed, they are
most **potent in potting**: your Dane, your German, and
your swag-bellied Hollander – Drink, ho! – are nothing
to your English.

CASSIO

Is your **Englishman so expert in his drinking?**

IAGO

Why, **he drinks you, with facility, your Dane dead
drunk**; he sweats not to overthrow your Almain; he
gives your Hollander a vomit, ere the next pottle
can be filled.

CASSIO

Gentlemen, let's look to our business.
Do not think, gentlemen, I am **drunk**: this is my
ancient; this is my right hand, and this is my left:
I am not drunk now; I can stand well enough, and
speak well enough.

ALL

Excellent well.

CASSIO

Why, very well then; you must not think then that **I am drunk**.

CASSIO

I will rather sue to be despised than to deceive so good a commander with so slight, so **drunken**, and so indiscreet an officer. **Drunk? and speak parrot? and squabble? swagger? swear?** and discourse fustian with one's own shadow? **O thou invisible spirit of wine, if thou hast no name to be known by, let us call thee devil!**

IAGO

What was he that you followed with your sword? What had he done to you?

CASSIO

I know not.

IAGO

Is't possible?

CASSIO

I remember a mass of things, but nothing distinctly;
a quarrel, but nothing wherefore. **O God, that men
should put an enemy in their mouths to steal away
their brains!** that we should, with joy, pleasance
revel and applause, transform ourselves into beasts!

IAGO

Why, but you are now well enough: how came you thus
recovered?

CASSIO

It hath pleased **the devil drunkenness** to give place
to the devil wrath; one unperfectness shows me
another, to make me frankly despise myself.

IAGO

Come, you are **too severe a moraler**: as the time,
the place, and the condition of this country
stands, I could heartily wish this had not befallen;
but, since it is as it is, mend it for your own good.

The Boozy Bard

CASSIO

I will ask him for my place again; he shall tell me
I am a **drunkard**! Had I as many mouths as Hydra,
such an answer would stop them all. To be now a
sensible man, by and by a fool, and presently a
beast! O strange! Every **inordinate cup** is
unblessed and **the ingredient is a devil**.

IAGO

Come, come, **good wine is a good familiar creature,
if it be well used**: exclaim no more against it.
And, good lieutenant, I think you think I love you.

CASSIO

I have well approved it, sir. I drunk!

IAGO

You or any man living may be drunk!

Act 2, Scene 3

EMILIA

He call'd her whore: a **beggar in his drink**
Could not have laid such terms upon his callat.

Act 4, Scene 2

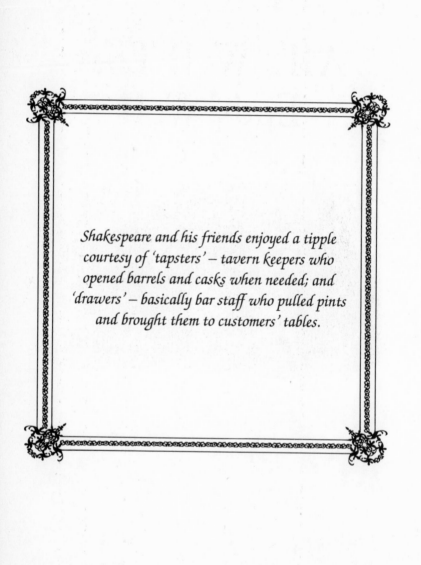

Shakespeare and his friends enjoyed a tipple
courtesy of 'tapsters' — tavern keepers who
opened barrels and casks when needed; and
'drawers' — basically bar staff who pulled pints
and brought them to customers' tables.

All's Well That Ends Well

PAROLLES

Drunkenness is his best virtue, for he will
be **swine-drunk**; and in his sleep he does little
harm, save to his bed-clothes about him.

Act 4, Scene 3

Antony and
Cleopatra

DOMITIUS ENOBARBUS

Bring in the banquet quickly; **wine** enough
Cleopatra's health to **drink**.

SOOTHSAYER

You shall be more beloving than beloved.

CHARMIAN

I had rather **heat my liver with drinking**.

Act 1, Scene 2

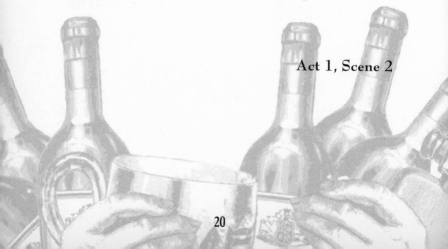

MECAENAS

You stayed well by 't in Egypt.

DOMITIUS ENOBARBUS

Ay, sir; we did sleep day out of countenance, and **made the night light with drinking.**

Act 2, Scene 2

MENAS

For my part, I am sorry it is turned to a **drinking**.
Pompey doth this day laugh away his fortune.

Act 2, Scene 6

FIRST SERVANT

Here they'll be, man. Some o' their plants are
ill-rooted already: the least wind i' the world
will blow them down.

SECOND SERVANT

Lepidus is high-coloured.

FIRST SERVANT

They have made him **drink alms-drink**.

SECOND SERVANT

As they pinch one another by the disposition, he
cries out 'No more;' **reconciles them to his
entreaty, and himself to the drink**.

POMPEY

Sit, – and **some wine**! A health to Lepidus!

LEPIDUS

I am not so well as I should be, but I'll ne'er out.

DOMITIUS ENOBARBUS

Not till you have slept; I fear me you'll be in till then.

POMPEY

This **wine** for Lepidus!

LEPIDUS

What manner o' thing is your crocodile?

MARK ANTONY

It is shaped, sir, like itself; and it is as broad
as it hath breadth: it is just so high as it is,
and moves with its own organs: it lives by that
which nourisheth it; and the elements once out of
it, it transmigrates...

OCTAVIUS CAESAR

Will this description satisfy him?

MARK ANTONY

With the health that Pompey gives him, else he is a very epicure.

POMPEY

Be **jolly**, lords.

MARK ANTONY

These quick-sands, Lepidus,
Keep off them, for you sink.

POMPEY

Desist, and drink.

POMPEY

Fill till the cup be hid.

DOMITIUS ENOBARBUS

Drink thou; increase the reels.

OCTAVIUS CAESAR

It's monstrous labour, when **I wash my brain**,
And it grows fouler.

MARK ANTONY

Be a child o' the time.

OCTAVIUS CAESAR

Possess it, I'll make answer:
But I had rather fast from all four days
Than **drink so much** in one.

DOMITIUS ENOBARBUS

Ha, my brave emperor!

To MARK ANTONY

Shall we dance now the **Egyptian Bacchanals**,
And **celebrate our drink**?

POMPEY

Let's ha't, good soldier.

MARK ANTONY

Come, let's all take hands,
Till that the **conquering wine** hath steep'd our sense
In soft and delicate Lethe.

Music plays. DOMITIUS ENOBARBUS places them hand in hand.

THE SONG.

Come, thou **monarch of the vine**,
Plumpy Bacchus with pink eyne!
In thy fats our cares be drown'd,
With thy grapes our hairs be crown'd:
Cup us, till the world go round,
Cup us, till the world go round!

OCTAVIUS CAESAR

What would you more? Pompey, good night. Good brother,
Let me request you off: our graver business
Frowns at this levity. Gentle lords, let's part;
You see we have **burnt our cheeks**: strong Enobarb
Is **weaker than the wine**; and **mine own tongue**
Splits what it speaks: the wild disguise hath almost
Antick'd us all. What needs more words? Good night.
Good Antony, your hand.

DOMITIUS ENOBARBUS

Take heed you fall not.

Act 2, Scene 7

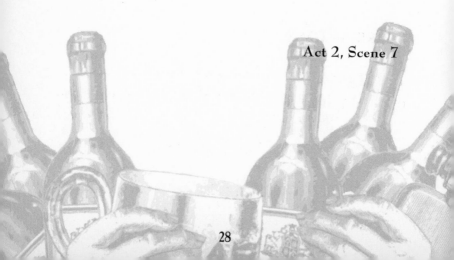

MARK ANTONY

... Come,
Let's have one other **gaudy night**: call to me
All my sad captains; **fill our bowls** once more;
Let's mock the midnight bell.

CLEOPATRA

It is my birth-day:
I had thought to have held it poor: but, since my lord
Is Antony again, I will be Cleopatra.

MARK ANTONY

We will yet do well.

CLEOPATRA

Call all his noble captains to my lord.

MARK ANTONY

Do so, we'll speak to them; and to-night I'll force
The wine peep through their scars. Come on, my queen;
There's sap in't yet.

Act 3, Scene 13

MARK ANTONY

I am dying, Egypt, dying:
Give me some wine, and let me speak a little.

Act 4, Scene 15

As You Like It

ROSALIND

I would thou couldst
stammer, that thou mightst pour this concealed man
out of thy mouth, **as wine comes out of a narrow-mouthed bottle**, either too much at once, or none at
all. I prithee, **take the cork out** of thy mouth that I
may **drink** thy tidings.

CELIA

So you may put a man in your belly.

Act 3, Scene 2

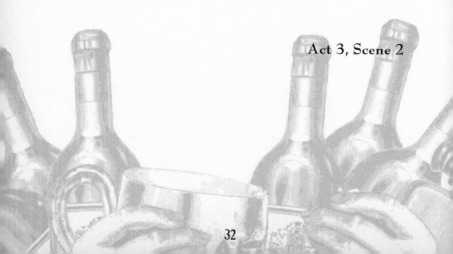

TOUCHSTONE

Then learn this of me: to have, is to have; for it
is a figure in rhetoric that **drink**, being poured out
of a cup **into a glass**, by filling the one doth empty
the other...

Act 5, Scene 1

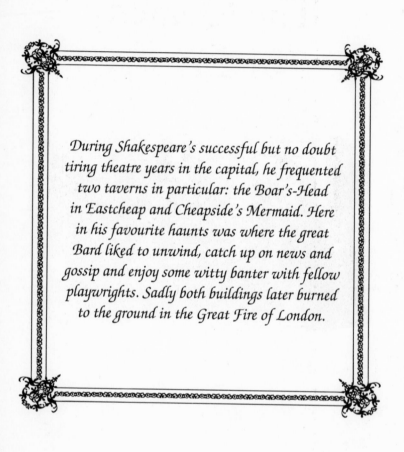

During Shakespeare's successful but no doubt
tiring theatre years in the capital, he frequented
two taverns in particular: the Boar's-Head
in Eastcheap and Cheapside's Mermaid. Here
in his favourite haunts was where the great
Bard liked to unwind, catch up on news and
gossip and enjoy some witty banter with fellow
playwrights. Sadly both buildings later burned
to the ground in the Great Fire of London.

The Comedy of Errors

ANTIPHOLUS OF EPHESUS

My liege, I am advised what I say,
Neither **disturbed with the effect of wine,**
Nor heady-rash, provoked with raging ire...

DUKE SOLINUS

Why, what an intricate impeach is this!
I think you all have **drunk of Circe's cup.**

Act 5, Scene 1

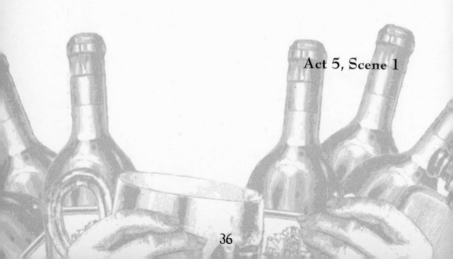

The Tragedy of Coriolanus

CORIOLANUS

I am weary; yea, my memory is tired.
Have we no **wine** here?

Act 1, Scene 9

MENENIUS

I am known to be a humorous patrician, and one that loves **a cup of hot wine with not a drop of allaying Tiber in't**; said to be something imperfect in favouring the first complaint; hasty and tinder-like upon too trivial motion; one that converses more with the buttock of the night than with the forehead of the morning: what I think I utter, and spend my malice in my breath. Meeting two such wealsmen as you are – I cannot call you Lycurguses – if the **drink** you give me touch my palate adversely, I make a crooked face at it.

Act 2, Scene 1

FIRST SERVINGMAN

Wine, wine, wine! What service
is here! I think our fellows are asleep.

Act 4, Scene 5

MENENIUS

He was not taken well; he had not dined:
The veins unfill'd, our blood is cold, and then
We pout upon the morning, are unapt
To give or to forgive; but when we have stuff'd
These pipes and these conveyances of our blood
With wine and feeding, we have suppler souls
Than in our priest-like fasts...

Act 5, Scene 1

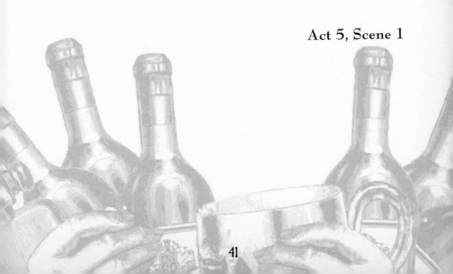

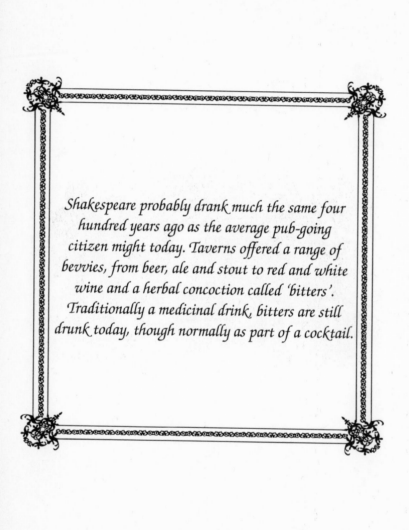

Shakespeare probably drank much the same four hundred years ago as the average pub-going citizen might today. Taverns offered a range of bevvies, from beer, ale and stout to red and white wine and a herbal concoction called 'bitters'. Traditionally a medicinal drink, bitters are still drunk today, though normally as part of a cocktail.

Cymbeline

The Boozy Bard

A British prison.

FIRST GAOLER

Come, sir, are you ready for death?

POSTHUMUS LEONATUS

Over-roasted rather; ready long ago.

FIRST GAOLER

Hanging is the word, sir: if
you be ready for that, you are well cooked.

POSTHUMUS LEONATUS

So, if I prove a good repast to the
spectators, the dish pays the shot.

FIRST GAOLER

A heavy reckoning for you, sir. But the comfort is,
you shall be called to no more payments, **fear no
more tavern-bills**; which are often the sadness of
parting, as the procuring of mirth: you come in
flint for want of meat, **depart reeling with too**

much drink; sorry that you have paid too much, and
sorry that you are paid too much; **purse and brain
both empty**; the brain the heavier for being too
light, the purse too light, being drawn of
heaviness: of this contradiction you shall now be
quit.

Act 5, Scene 4

The Friday Street Club was set up by Sir Walter Raleigh and met every Friday, on Friday Street, in the Mermaid tavern. Here poets, playwrights and actors including Raleigh, Shakespeare, John Donne, Sir Francis Bacon and Ben Jonson gathered together for convivial evenings, where sack and ale surely flowed. Shakespeare and Jonson are said to have provided much of the entertainment with their ongoing verbal locking of horns. While Jonson's intellect was unquestionable, it is said that Shakespeare's quick wit proclaimed him victor over and over again.

Hamlet

HAMLET

But what is your affair in Elsinore?
We'll teach you to **drink deep** ere you depart.

HORATIO

My lord, I came to see your father's funeral.

HAMLET

I pray thee, do not mock me, fellow-student;
I think it was to see my mother's wedding.

Act 1, Scene 2

LORD POLONIUS

But, sir, such wanton, wild and usual slips
As are companions noted and most known
To youth and liberty.

REYNALDO

As gaming, my lord.

LORD POLONIUS

Ay, or **drinking**, fencing, swearing, quarrelling,
Drabbing: you may go so far.

Act 2, Scene 1

KING CLAUDIUS

Set me the stoops of wine upon that table.
If Hamlet give the first or second hit,
Or quit in answer of the third exchange,
Let all the battlements their ordnance fire:
The king shall **drink** to Hamlet's better breath.

QUEEN GERTRUDE

He's fat, and scant of breath.
Here, Hamlet, take my napkin, rub thy brows;
The queen carouses to thy fortune, Hamlet.

HAMLET

Good madam!

KING CLAUDIUS

Gertrude, **do not drink.**

QUEEN GERTRUDE

I will, my lord; I pray you, pardon me.

HAMLET

How does the queen?

KING CLAUDIUS

She swounds to see them bleed.

QUEEN GERTRUDE

No, no, **the drink, the drink,** – O my dear Hamlet, –
The drink, the drink! I am poison'd.

Act 5, Scene 2

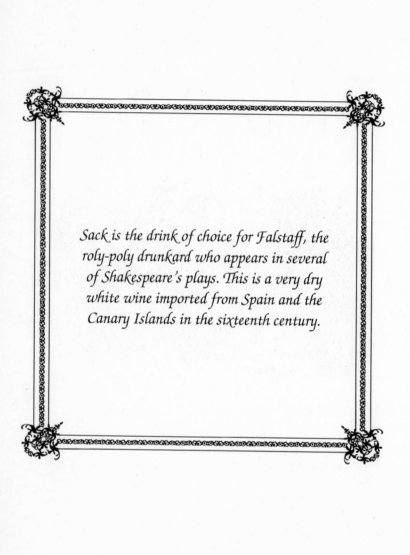

Sack is the drink of choice for Falstaff, the roly-poly drunkard who appears in several of Shakespeare's plays. This is a very dry white wine imported from Spain and the Canary Islands in the sixteenth century.

Henry IV, Part I

The Boozy Bard

FALSTAFF

Now, Hal, what time of day is it, lad?

PRINCE HENRY

Thou art so fat-witted, with **drinking of old sack** and unbuttoning thee after supper and sleeping upon benches after noon, that thou hast forgotten to demand that truly which thou wouldst truly know. What a devil hast thou to do with the time of the day? **Unless hours were cups of sack** and minutes capons and clocks the tongues of bawds and dials the signs of leaping-houses and the blessed sun himself a fair hot wench in flame-coloured taffeta...

FALSTAFF

... And is not **my hostess of the tavern** a most sweet wench?

PRINCE HENRY

Why, what a pox have I to do with my hostess of the tavern?

FALSTAFF

Well, thou hast called her to a reckoning many a
time and oft.

PRINCE HENRY

Did I ever call for thee to pay thy part?

FALSTAFF

No; I'll give thee thy due, thou hast paid all there.

POINS

Good morrow, sweet Hal. What says Monsieur
Remorse?
what says Sir John Sack and Sugar? Jack! how
agrees the devil and thee about thy soul, that thou
soldest him on Good-Friday last for **a cup of Madeira**
and a cold capon's leg?

Act 1, Scene 2

GADSHILL

I am joined with no
foot-land rakers, no long-staff sixpenny strikers,
none of these **mad mustachio purple-hued malt-worms;**
but with nobility and tranquillity, burgomasters and
great oneyers, such as can hold in, such as will
strike sooner than speak, and **speak sooner than
drink, and drink sooner than pray...**

Act 2, Scene 1

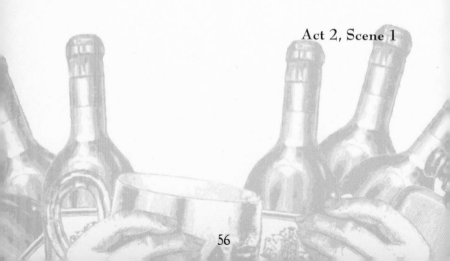

FALSTAFF

… An I
have not ballads made on you all and sung to filthy
tunes, **let a cup of sack be my poison**: when a jest
is so forward, and afoot too! I hate it.

Act 2, Scene 2

The Boozy Bard

The Boar's-Head Tavern, Eastcheap.

PRINCE HENRY

Sirrah, I am sworn brother
to a leash of drawers; and can call them all by
their christen names, as Tom, Dick, and Francis.
... **They call drinking deep, dyeing
scarlet; and when you breathe in your watering, they
cry 'hem!'** and bid you play it off. To conclude, I
am so good a proficient in one quarter of an hour,
that **I can drink with any tinker** in his own language
during my life… 'Anon, anon, sir! **Score a pint
of bastard in the Half-Moon,'** or so.

PRINCE HENRY

Sirrah, Falstaff and the rest of the thieves are at
the door: shall we be merry?

POINS

As merry as crickets, my lad.

FALSTAFF

Give me a cup of sack, boy. Ere I lead this life long, I'll sew nether stocks and mend
them and foot them too. A plague of all cowards!
Give me a cup of sack, rogue. Is there no virtue extant?

He drinks.

FALSTAFF

You rogue, here's lime in this sack too: there is nothing but roguery to be found in villanous man: yet a coward is worse than a cup of sack with lime in it. A villanous coward!

FALSTAFF

Give me a cup of sack: I am a rogue, if I
drunk to-day.

PRINCE HENRY

O villain! thy lips are scarce wiped since thou
drunkest last.

FALSTAFF

Well, an the fire of grace be not quite out of thee,
now shalt thou be moved. Give me a cup of sack to
make my eyes look red, that it may be thought I have
wept; for I must speak in passion, and I will do it
in King Cambyses' vein.

FALSTAFF

If sack and sugar be a fault,
God help the wicked! if to be old and merry be a
sin, then many an old host that I know is damned...

PETO

Falstaff! — Fast asleep behind the arras, and
snorting like a horse.

PRINCE HENRY

Hark, how hard he fetches breath. Search his pockets.
He searcheth his pockets, and findeth certain papers
What hast thou found?

PETO

Nothing but papers, my lord.

PRINCE HENRY

Let's see what they be: read them.

PETO

[Reads] Item, A capon,... 2s. 2d.
Item, Sauce,... 4d.
Item, Sack, two gallons, 5s. 8d.

Item, Anchovies and sack after supper, 2s. 6d.
Item, Bread, ob.

PRINCE HENRY

O monstrous! but one half-penny-worth of bread to
this intolerable deal of sack!

Act 2, Scene 4

Henry IV, Part II

The Boozy Bard

The Boar's-Head Tavern, Eastcheap.

MISTRESS QUICKLY

But, i' faith, **you have drunk too much canaries; and that's a marvellous searching wine,** and it perfumes the blood ere one can say 'What's this?' How do you now?

DOLL TEARSHEET

Better than I was: 'hem!

DOLL TEARSHEET OF FALSTAFF:

Can a weak empty vessel bear such a huge full hogshead? **there's a whole merchant's venture of Bourdeaux stuff in him;** you have not seen a hulk better stuffed in the hold.

FALSTAFF

Welcome, Ancient Pistol. Here, Pistol, I charge
you with **a cup of sack**: do you discharge upon mine
hostess.

PISTOL

I will discharge upon her, Sir John, with two bullets.

FALSTAFF

She is Pistol-proof, sir; you shall hardly offend
her.

MISTRESS QUICKLY

Come, I'll drink no proofs nor no bullets: **I'll
drink no more than will do me good**, for no man's
pleasure, I.

PISTOL

Then to you, Mistress Dorothy; I will charge you.

DOLL TEARSHEET

Charge me! I scorn you, scurvy companion. What!

you poor, base, rascally, cheating, lack-linen
mate! Away, you mouldy rogue, away! I am meat for
your master.

PISTOL

I know you, Mistress Dorothy.

DOLL TEARSHEET

Away, you cut-purse rascal! you filthy bung, away!
by this wine, I'll thrust my knife in your mouldy
chaps, an you play the saucy cuttle with me. Away,
you **bottle-ale rascal**! you basket-hilt stale
juggler, you!

Act 2, Scene 4

FALSTAFF

Come, **I will go drink with you**, but I cannot tarry dinner.

Act 3, Scene 2

LANCASTER

Let's **drink together friendly** and embrace,
That all their eyes may bear those tokens home
Of our restored love and amity.

Act 4, Scene 2

FALSTAFF

Good faith, this same young sober-
blooded boy doth not love me; **nor a man cannot make
him laugh; but that's no marvel, he drinks no wine.**
There's never none of these demure boys come to any
proof; for **thin drink doth so over-cool their blood,**
and making many fish-meals, that they fall into a
kind of male green-sickness; and then when they
marry, they get wenches: they are generally fools
and cowards; which some of us should be too, but for
inflammation. **A good sherris sack hath a two-fold
operation in it.** It ascends me into the brain;
dries me there all the foolish and dull and curdy
vapours which environ it; makes it apprehensive,
quick, forgetive, full of nimble fiery and
delectable shapes, which, delivered o'er to the
voice, the tongue, which is the birth, becomes
excellent wit. **The second property of your
excellent sherris** is, the warming of the blood;
which, before cold and settled, left the liver
white and pale, which is the badge of pusillanimity
and cowardice; but **the sherris warms it** and makes
it course from the inwards to the parts extreme:
it illumineth the face, which as a beacon gives
warning to all the rest of this little kingdom,
man, to arm; and then the vital commoners and

inland petty spirits muster me all to their captain,
the heart, who, great and puffed up with this
retinue, doth any deed of courage; and **this valour
comes of sherris.** So that skill in the weapon is
nothing without sack, for that sets it a-work; and
learning a mere hoard of gold kept by a devil, till
sack commences it and sets it in act and use.
Hereof comes it that Prince Harry is valiant; for
**the cold blood he did naturally inherit of his
father, he hath, like lean, sterile and bare land,
manured, husbanded and tilled with excellent
endeavour of drinking good and good store of fertile
sherris,** that he is become very hot and valiant. If
I had a thousand sons, the first humane principle I
would teach them should be, to forswear thin
potations and to **addict themselves to sack.**

Act 4, Scene 3

SHALLOW

Sir John: by the mass, **I have drunk too much sack at supper:** a good varlet. Now sit down, now sit down: come, cousin.

SILENCE

Ah, sirrah! quoth-a, we shall
Do nothing but eat, and make **good cheer,**
[Singing] And praise God for the merry year;
When flesh is cheap and females dear,
And lusty lads roam here and there
So merrily,
And ever among so merrily.

FALSTAFF

There's a merry heart! Good Master Silence, I'll give you a health for that anon.

SHALLOW

Give Master Bardolph some wine, Davy.

DAVY

Sweet sir, sit; I'll be with you anon. most sweet

sir, sit. Master page, good master page, sit.
Proface! **What you want in meat, we'll have in drink:**
but you must bear; the heart's all.

DAVY

[To BARDOLPH] A cup of wine, sir?

SILENCE

[Singing] **A cup of wine that's brisk and fine,**
And drink unto the leman mine;
And **a merry heart lives long-a.**

FALSTAFF

Well said, Master Silence.

SILENCE

**An we shall be merry, now comes in the sweet o' the
night.**

FALSTAFF

Health and long life to you, Master Silence.

SILENCE

Fill the cup, and let it come;
[Singing] I'll pledge you a mile to the bottom.

Act 5, Scene 3

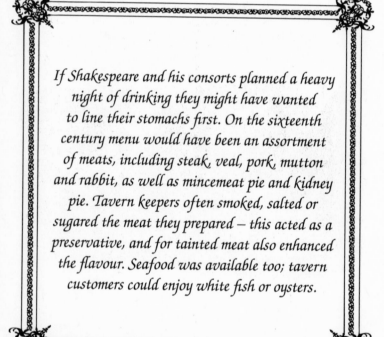

If Shakespeare and his consorts planned a heavy night of drinking they might have wanted to line their stomachs first. On the sixteenth century menu would have been an assortment of meats, including steak, veal, pork, mutton and rabbit, as well as mincemeat pie and kidney pie. Tavern keepers often smoked, salted or sugared the meat they prepared — this acted as a preservative, and for tainted meat also enhanced the flavour. Seafood was available too; tavern customers could enjoy white fish or oysters.

Henry V

BISHOP OF ELY

This would **drink deep.**

ARCHBISHOP OF CANTERBURY

'Twould drink the cup and all.

Act 1, Scene 1

KING HENRY V

Enlarge the man committed yesterday,
That rail'd against our person: we consider
it was **excess of wine** that set him on;
And on his more advice we pardon him.

Act 2, Scene 2

CONSTABLE

Dieu de batailles! where have they this mettle?
Is not their climate foggy, raw and dull,
On whom, as in despite, the sun looks pale,
Killing their fruit with frowns? Can sodden water,
A drench for sur-rein'd jades, their **barley-broth**,
Decoct their cold blood to such valiant heat?
And shall our quick blood, **spirited with wine**,
Seem frosty?

Act 3, Scene 5

Henry V

KING HENRY V

… then shall our names.
Familiar in his mouth as household words
Harry the king, Bedford and Exeter,
Warwick and Talbot, Salisbury and Gloucester,
Be in their **flowing cups** freshly remember'd.

Act 4, Scene 3

FLUELLEN

Alexander killed his friend Cleitus, **being in his ales and his cups.**

Act 4, Scene 7

Henry VI, Part I

TALBOT [To COUNTESS OF AUVERGNE]

Nor other satisfaction do I crave,
But only, with your patience, that we may
Taste of your wine and see what cates you have;
For soldiers' stomachs always serve them well.

Act 2, Scene 3

Henry VI, Part II

The Boozy Bard

FIRST NEIGHBOUR

Here, neighbour Horner, **I drink to you in a cup of
sack**: and fear not, neighbour, you shall do well enough.

SECOND NEIGHBOUR

And here, neighbour, here's a cup of charneco.

THIRD NEIGHBOUR

And here's **a pot of good double beer**, neighbour:
drink, and fear not your man.

PETER

I thank you all: **drink, and pray for me, I pray
you; for I think I have taken my last draught in
this world.** Here, Robin, an if I die, I give thee
my apron: and, Will, thou shalt have my hammer:
and here, Tom, take all the money that I have.

Act 2, Scene 3

QUEEN MARGARET

Is all thy comfort shut in Gloucester's tomb?
Why, then, dame Margaret was ne'er thy joy.
Erect his statue and worship it,
And make my image but **an alehouse sign**.

Act 3, Scene 2

CARDINAL

Give me some drink; and bid the apothecary
Bring the strong poison that I bought of him.

Act 3, Scene 3

CADE

Be brave, then; for your captain is brave, and vows
reformation. There shall be in England seven
halfpenny loaves sold for a penny: the three-hooped
pot shall have ten hoops; and **I will make it felony
to drink small beer**: all the realm shall be in
common; and in Cheapside shall my palfrey go to
grass: and when I am king, as king I will be, –

ALL

God save your majesty!

CADE

I thank you, good people: there shall be no money;
all shall eat and drink on my score; and I will
apparel them all in one livery, that they may agree
like brothers and worship me their lord.

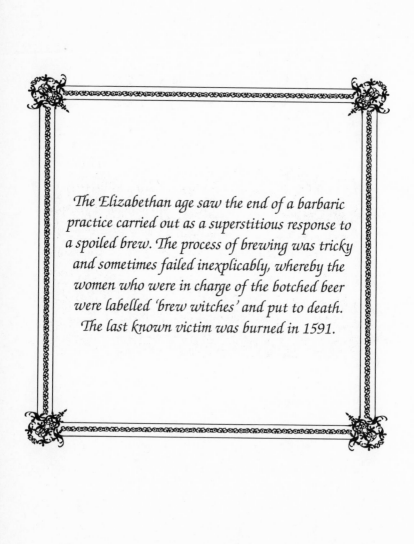

The Elizabethan age saw the end of a barbaric practice carried out as a superstitious response to a spoiled brew. The process of brewing was tricky and sometimes failed inexplicably, whereby the women who were in charge of the botched beer were labelled 'brew witches' and put to death. The last known victim was burned in 1591.

Henry VIII

The Boozy Bard

GUILDFORD

Ladies, a general welcome from his grace
Salutes ye all; this night he dedicates
To fair content and you: none here, he hopes,
In all this noble bevy, has brought with her
One care abroad; he would have all as merry
As, first, good company, **good wine**, good welcome,
Can make good people.

CARDINAL WOLSEY

My Lord Sands,
I am beholding to you: cheer your neighbours.
Ladies, you are not merry: gentlemen,
Whose fault is this?

SANDS

The **red wine first must rise
In their fair cheeks**, my lord; then we shall have 'em
Talk us to silence.

Henry VIII

KING HENRY VIII

Good my lord cardinal, I have **half a dozen healths**
To drink to these fair ladies...

Act 1, Scene 4

PORTER

Do you look for **ale and cakes** here, you rude rascals?

Act 5, Scene 4

Troilus and
Cressida

ULYSSES

I have derision medicinable,
To use between your strangeness and his pride,
Which his own will **shall have desire to drink**…

Act 3, Scene 3

ACHILLES

I'll heat his blood with Greekish wine to-night,
Which with my scimitar I'll cool to-morrow.
Patroclus, let us feast him to the height.

Act 5, Scene 1

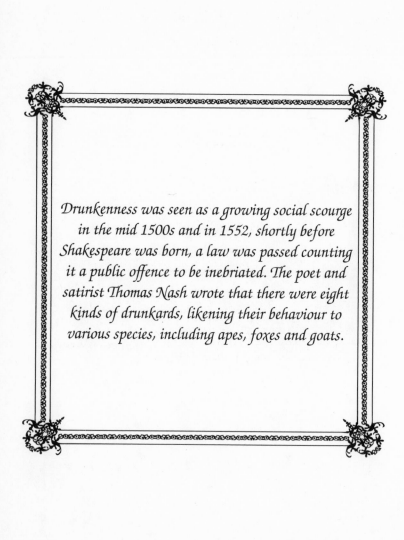

Drunkenness was seen as a growing social scourge in the mid 1500s and in 1552, shortly before Shakespeare was born, a law was passed counting it a public offence to be inebriated. The poet and satirist Thomas Nash wrote that there were eight kinds of drunkards, likening their behaviour to various species, including apes, foxes and goats.

Julius Caesar

CAESAR

Good friends, go in and **taste some wine with me**,
And we like friends will straightway go together.

Act 2, Scene 2

Re-enter LUCIUS, with wine and taper

BRUTUS

Speak no more of her. Give me **a bowl of wine**.
In this I bury all unkindness, Cassius.

CASSIUS

My heart is thirsty for that noble pledge.
Fill, Lucius, till the wine o'erswell the cup;
I cannot drink too much of Brutus' love.

Act 4, Scene 3

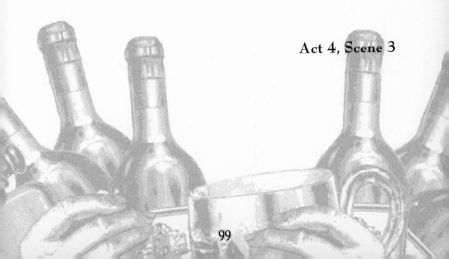

The bubonic plague that hit England in the sixteenth and seventeenth centuries originally infected rats. The so-called Black Death spread rapidly among the human population after they came into contact with fleas that had been feasting on the disease-ridden rodents. Victims found painful, swollen lymph nodes, usually around the groin to begin with, and skin gradually turned black. The inevitable outcome in nearly all cases was death.

Understandably, finding people to load the numerous bodies onto death carts for burial was a tough task, and the main incentive for these labourers was a substantial stock of alcohol.

King Lear

FOOL

> Leave **thy drink** and thy whore,
> And keep in-a-door,
> And thou shalt have more
> Than two tens to a score.

Act 1, Scene 4

King Richard II

JOHN OF GAUNT

O, spare me not, my brother Edward's son,
For that I was his father Edward's son;
That blood already, like the pelican,
Hast thou tapp'd out and **drunkenly caroused**...

Act 2, Scene 1

The Life and Death
of Richard III

GLOUCESTER

Plots have I laid, inductions dangerous,
By **drunken prophecies**, libels and dreams...

Act 1, Scene 1

CLARENCE

Where art thou, keeper? give me **a cup of wine.**

SECOND MURDERER

You shall have **wine enough,** my lord, anon.

Act 1, Scene 4

HASTINGS

O momentary grace of mortal men,
Which we more hunt for than the grace of God!
Who builds his hopes in air of your good looks,
Lives **like a drunken sailor on a mast,**
Ready, with every nod, to tumble down
Into the fatal bowels of the deep.

Act 3, Scene 5

KING RICHARD III

So, I am satisfied. **Give me a bowl of wine:**
I have not that alacrity of spirit,
Nor cheer of mind, that I was wont to have.
Set it down. Is ink and paper ready?

GHOST OF CLARENCE

[To KING RICHARD III] Let me sit heavy on thy soul
to-morrow!
I, that was wash'd to death with fulsome wine,
Poor Clarence, by thy guile betrayed to death!

Act 5, Scene 3

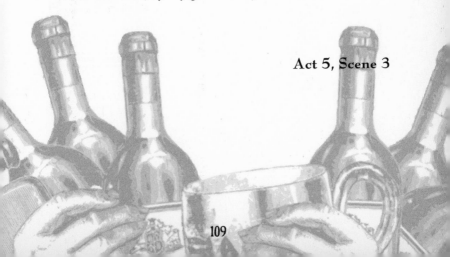

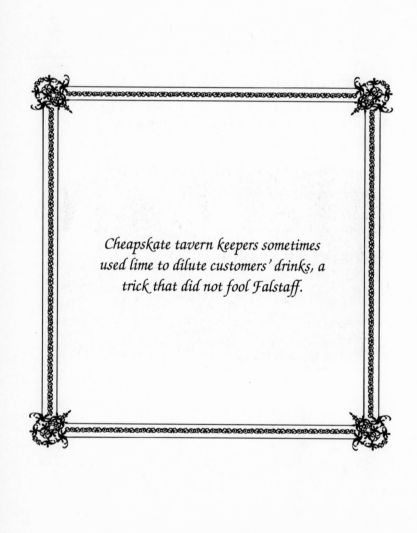

Cheapskate tavern keepers sometimes used lime to dilute customers' drinks, a trick that did not fool Falstaff.

Timon of Athens

SECOND LORD

Thou art going to Lord Timon's feast?

APEMANTUS

Ay, to see meat fill knaves and wine heat fools.

Act 1, Scene 1

APEMANTUS

I wonder men dare trust themselves with men:
Methinks they should invite them without knives;
Good for their meat, and safer for their lives.
There's much example for't; the fellow that sits
next him now, parts bread with him, **pledges the
breath of him in a divided draught**, is the readiest
man to kill him: 't has been proved. If I were a
huge man, **I should fear to drink at meals;**
Lest they should spy my windpipe's dangerous notes:
**Great men should drink with harness on their
throats.**

TIMON

Mine eyes cannot hold out water, methinks: to
forget their faults, **I drink to you.**

APEMANTUS

Thou weepest to make them drink, Timon.

APEMANTUS

We make ourselves fools, to disport ourselves;
And spend our flatteries, **to drink** those men
Upon whose age we void it up again,
With poisonous spite and envy.

Act 2, Scene 2

FLAVIUS

... our vaults have wept
With drunken spilth of wine, when every room
Hath blazed with lights and bray'd with minstrelsy...

Act 2, Scene 2

FIRST STRANGER

... nay, Timon's money
Has paid his men their wages: **he ne'er drinks,**
But Timon's silver treads upon his lip;
And yet – O, see the monstrousness of man
When he looks out in an ungrateful shape!

Act 3, Scene 2

SECOND SENATOR

He has been known to commit outrages,
And cherish factions: 'tis inferr'd to us,
His days are foul and **his drink dangerous.**

Act 3, Scene 5

APEMANTUS

Thy flatterers yet wear silk, **drink wine**, lie soft…

Will the cold brook,
Candied with ice, caudle thy morning taste,
To cure thy **o'er-night's surfeit**?

Act 4, Scene 3

Love's Labour's Lost

BIRON

One drunkard loves another of the name.

Act 4, Scene 3

Macbeth

The Boozy Bard

LADY MACBETH

Was the hope drunk
Wherein you dress'd yourself? hath it slept since?
And wakes it now, to look so green and pale
At what it did so freely?

LADY MACBETH

But screw your courage to the sticking-place,
And we'll not fail. When Duncan is asleep –
Whereto the rather shall his day's hard journey
Soundly invite him – his two chamberlains
Will I with wine and wassail so convince
That memory, the warder of the brain,
Shall be a fume, and the receipt of reason
A limbeck only: when in swinish sleep
Their drenched natures lie as in a death,
What cannot you and I perform upon
The unguarded Duncan?

Act 1, Scene 7

MACBETH

Go bid thy mistress, **when my drink is ready**,
She strike upon the bell. Get thee to bed.

Act 2, Scene 1

LADY MACBETH

That which hath made them **drunk** hath made me bold;
What hath quench'd them hath given me fire.
Hark! Peace!
It was the owl that shriek'd, the fatal bellman,
Which gives the stern'st good-night. He is about it:
The doors are open; and **the surfeited grooms**
Do mock their charge with snores.

Act 2, Scene 2

Macbeth

MACDUFF

Was it so late, friend, ere you went to bed,
That you do lie so late?

PORTER

Faith sir, **we were carousing** till the
second cock: and **drink**, sir, is a great
provoker of three things.

MACDUFF

What three things does drink especially provoke?

PORTER

Marry, sir, nose-painting, sleep, and
urine. Lechery, sir, it provokes, and unprovokes;
it provokes the desire, but it takes
away the performance: therefore, **much drink
may be said to be an equivocator with lechery**:
it makes him, and it mars him; it sets
him on, and it takes him off; it persuades him,
and disheartens him; makes him stand to, and
not stand to; in conclusion, equivocates him
in a sleep, and, giving him the lie, leaves him.

The Boozy Bard

MACDUFF

I believe **drink gave thee the lie** last night.

PORTER

That it did, sir, i' the very throat on
me: but I requited him for his lie; and, I
think, being too strong for him, though he took
up my legs sometime, yet I made a shift to cast
him.

MACBETH

... from this instant,
There's nothing serious in mortality:
All is but toys: renown and grace is dead;
**The wine of life is drawn, and the mere lees
Is left this vault to brag of.**

Act 2, Scene 3

MACBETH

Be large in mirth; anon **we'll drink a measure**
The table round.

... Give me some wine; fill full.
I drink to the general joy o' the whole table.

Act 3, Scene 4

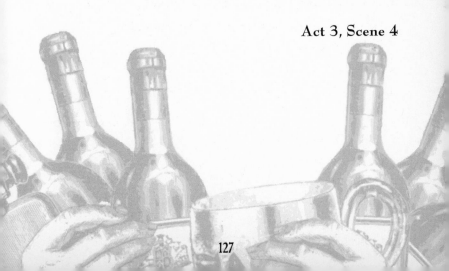

LENNOX

How it did grieve Macbeth! did he not straight
In pious rage the two delinquents tear,
That were **the slaves of drink** and thralls of sleep?

Act 3, Scene 6

Measure for Measure

ELBOW

Nay, if there be no remedy for it, but that you will
needs buy and sell men and women like beasts, **we
shall have all the world drink brown and white
bastard**.

LUCIO

A little more lenity to lechery would do no harm in
him: something too crabbed that way, friar.

DUKE VINCENTIO

It is too general a vice, and severity must cure it.

LUCIO

Yes, in good sooth, the vice is of a great kindred;
it is well allied: but it is impossible to extirp
it quite, friar, till eating and **drinking** be put
down.

Act 3, Scene 2

DUKE VINCENTIO

Hath he born himself penitently in prison? How
seems he to be touched?

PROVOST

A man that apprehends death no more dreadfully but
as **a drunken sleep**; careless, reckless, and fearless
of what's past, present, or to come; insensible of
mortality, and desperately mortal.

DUKE VINCENTIO

He wants advice.

PROVOST

He will hear none: he hath evermore had the liberty
of the prison; give him leave to escape hence, he
would not: **drunk many times a day, if not many days
entirely drunk.** We have very oft awaked him, as if
to carry him to execution, and showed him a seeming
warrant for it: it hath not moved him at all.

Act 4, Scene 2

BARNARDINE

You rogue, I have been drinking all night; I am not fitted for 't.

POMPEY

O, the better, sir; for **he that drinks all night**, and is hanged betimes in the morning, may sleep the sounder all the next day.

Act 4, Scene 3

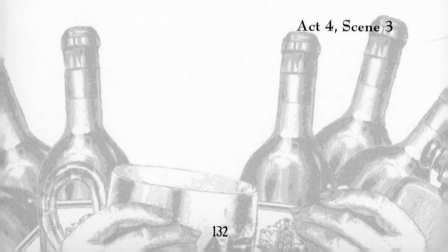

The Merchant
of Venice

NERISSA

How like you the young German, the Duke of Saxony's nephew?

PORTIA

Very vilely in the morning, when he is **sober**, and most vilely in the afternoon, when he is **drunk**: when he is best, he is a little worse than a man, and when he is worst, he is little better than a beast.

Act 1, Scene 1

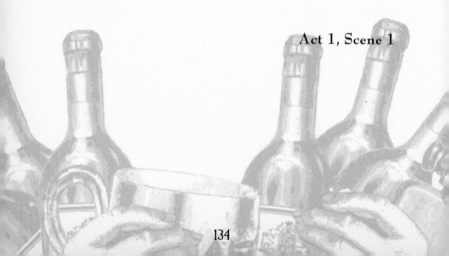

SHYLOCK

I will buy with you, sell with you, talk with you,
walk with you, and so following, but I will not eat
with you, **drink with you**, nor pray with you.

Act 1, Scene 3

SHYLOCK

I say, my daughter is my flesh and blood.

SALARINO

There is more difference between thy flesh and hers than between jet and ivory; more between your bloods than there is between **red wine and rhenish**.

Act 3, Scene 1

The Merry Wives of Windsor

The Boozy Bard

SLENDER

By this hat, then, he in the red face had it; for
though I cannot remember what I did when you made
me
drunk, yet I am not altogether an ass.

FALSTAFF

What say you, Scarlet and John?

BARDOLPH

Why, sir, for my part I say the gentleman had **drunk
himself out of his five sentences**.

SIR HUGH EVANS

It is his five senses: fie, what the ignorance is!

BARDOLPH

And being fap, sir, was, as they say, cashiered; and
so conclusions passed the careires.

SLENDER

Ay, you spake in Latin then too; but 'tis no

matter: **I'll ne'er be drunk** whilst I live again,
but in honest, civil, godly company, for this trick:
**if I be drunk, I'll be drunk with those that have
the fear of God, and not with drunken knaves.**

PAGE

Wife, bid these gentlemen welcome. Come, we have a
hot venison pasty to dinner: come, gentlemen, I hope
we shall drink down all unkindness.

Act 1, Scene 1

NYM

He was gotten in **drink**. Is not the humour conceited?

Act 1, Scene 3

MISTRESS PAGE

What, have I scaped love-letters in the holiday –
time of my beauty, and am I now a subject for them?
Let me see.
[Reads] 'Ask me no reason why I love you; for though
Love use Reason for his physician, he admits him
not for his counsellor. You are not young, no more
am I; go to then, there's sympathy: **you are merry,**
so am I; ha, ha! then there's more sympathy: **you
love sack,** and so do I; **would you desire better
sympathy?...**'
... What an
unweighed behaviour hath this Flemish drunkard
picked – with the devil's name! – out of my
conversation, that he dares in this manner assay me?

Act 2, Scene 1

HOST

Farewell, my hearts: I will to my honest knight
Falstaff, and **drink canary** with him.

FORD

[Aside] I think I shall drink in **pipe wine** first
with him; I'll make him dance. Will you go, gentles?

Act 3, Scene 2

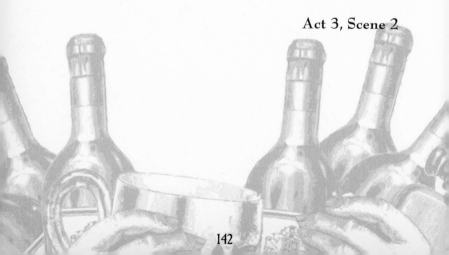

SIR HUGH EVANS

And given to fornications, and **to taverns and sack and wine and metheglins, and to drinkings** and swearings and starings, pribbles and prabbles?

FALSTAFF

Well, I am your theme: you have the start of me.

Act 5, Scene 5

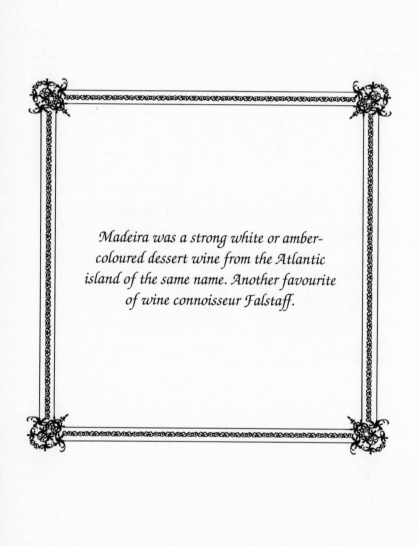

Madeira was a strong white or amber-coloured dessert wine from the Atlantic island of the same name. Another favourite of wine connoisseur Falstaff.

A Midsummer Night's Dream

PUCK

And sometime lurk I in a gossip's bowl,
In very likeness of a roasted crab,
And when she **drinks**, against her lips I bob
And on her wither'd dewlap pour the **ale**.

Act 2, Scene 1

Much Ado About Nothing

BENEDICK

With anger, with sickness, or with hunger, my lord,
not with love: prove that ever I lose more blood
with love than I will get again with **drinking**, pick
out mine eyes with a ballad-maker's pen and hang me
up at the door of a brothel-house for the sign of
blind Cupid.

Act 1, Scene 1

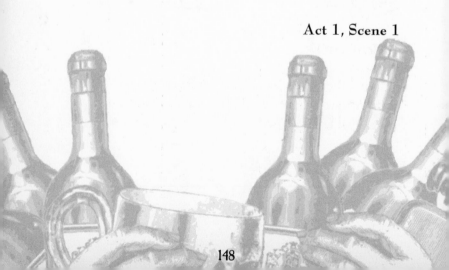

DOGBERRY

Why, you speak like an ancient and most quiet watchman; for I cannot see how sleeping should offend: only, have a care that your bills be not stolen. Well, you are to call at all the **ale-houses**, and bid those that are **drunk** get them to bed.

WATCHMAN

How if they will not?

DOGBERRY

Why, then, let them alone till they are **sober**: if they make you not then the better answer, you may say they are not the men you took them for.

BORACHIO

Stand thee close, then, under this pent-house, for it drizzles rain; and I will, **like a true drunkard,** utter all to thee.

Act 3, Scene 3

LEONATO

Drink some wine ere you go: fare you well.

Act 3, Scene 5

LEONATO

Patch grief with proverbs, make misfortune **drunk**
With candle-wasters...

Act 5, Scene 1

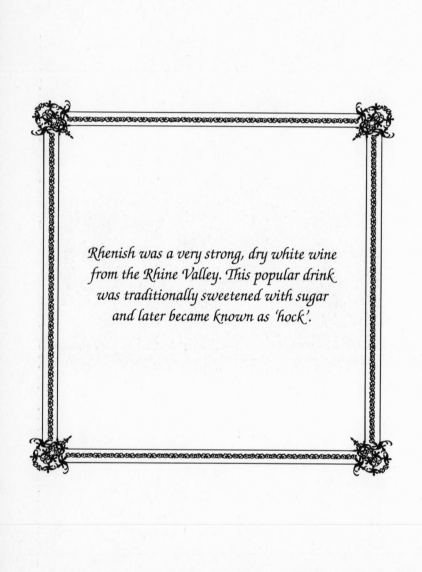

Rhenish was a very strong, dry white wine
from the Rhine Valley. This popular drink
was traditionally sweetened with sugar
and later became known as 'hock'.

Pericles

SECOND FISHERMAN

What a drunken knave was the sea to cast thee in our way!

Act 2, Scene 1

SIMONIDES

Here, with a cup that's stored unto the brim, —
As you do love, fill to your mistress' lips, —
We drink this health to you.

SIMONIDES

Here, say we **drink this standing-bowl of wine** to him.

THAISA

The king my father, sir, has drunk to you.

PERICLES

I thank him.

THAISA

Wishing it so much blood unto your life.

PERICLES

I thank both him and you, and pledge him freely.

Act 2, Scene 3

Romeo and Juliet

SERVANT

Now I'll tell you without asking: my master is the
great rich Capulet; and if you be not of the house
of Montagues, I pray, come and **crush a cup of wine**.
Rest you merry!

Act 1, Scene 2

FRIAR LAURENCE

The grey-eyed morn smiles on the frowning night,
Chequering the eastern clouds with streaks of light,
And flecked darkness **like a drunkard** reels
From forth day's path and Titan's fiery wheels…

Act 2, Scene 3

MERCUTIO

Thou art like one of those fellows that when he
enters the confines of a **tavern** claps me his sword
upon the table and says 'God send me no need of
thee!' and **by the operation of the second cup** draws
it on the drawer, when indeed there is no need.

Act 3, Scene 1

NURSE

O holy friar, O, tell me, holy friar,
Where is my lady's lord, where's Romeo?

FRIAR LAURENCE

There on the ground, with his own tears made **drunk**.

Act 3, Scene 3

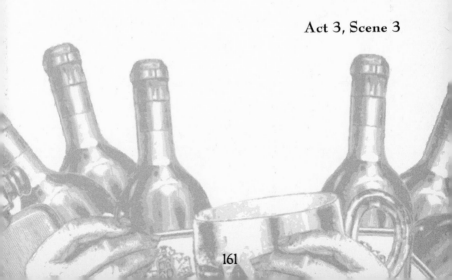

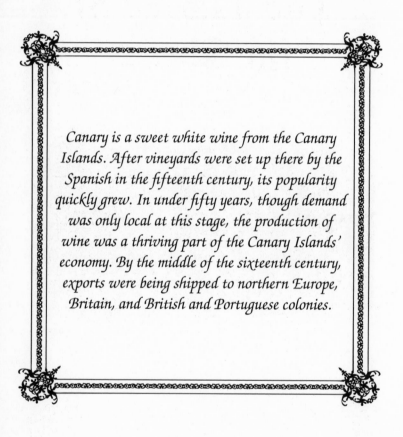

Canary is a sweet white wine from the Canary Islands. After vineyards were set up there by the Spanish in the fifteenth century, its popularity quickly grew. In under fifty years, though demand was only local at this stage, the production of wine was a thriving part of the Canary Islands' economy. By the middle of the sixteenth century, exports were being shipped to northern Europe, Britain, and British and Portuguese colonies.

The Taming of
the Shrew

The Boozy Bard

Before an alehouse on a heath.

HOSTESS

You will not pay for the glasses you have burst?

SLY

No, not a denier. Go by, Jeronimy: go to thy cold
bed, and warm thee.
Falls asleep.

LORD

What's here? one **dead, or drunk**? See, doth he
breathe?

SECOND HUNTSMAN

He breathes, my lord. Were he not **warm'd with ale**,
This were a bed but cold to sleep so soundly.

The Taming of the Shrew

LORD

O monstrous beast! how like a swine he lies!
Grim death, how foul and loathsome is thine image!
Sirs, I will practise on this drunken man.
What think you, if he were convey'd to bed,
Wrapp'd in sweet clothes, rings put upon his fingers,
A most delicious banquet by his bed,
And brave attendants near him when he wakes,
Would not the beggar then forget himself?

Sirrah, go you to Barthol'mew my page,
And see him dress'd in all suits like a lady:
That done, conduct him to the **drunkard**'s chamber;
And call him 'madam', do him obeisance.
... Such duty to the **drunkard** let him do
With soft low tongue and lowly courtesy,
And say 'What is't your honour will command,
Wherein your lady and your humble wife
May show her duty and make known her love?'

Induction, Scene 1

SLY

For God's sake, **a pot of small ale.**

FIRST SERVANT

Will't please your lordship drink **a cup of sack**?

SECOND SERVANT

Will't please your honour taste of these conserves?

THIRD SERVANT

What raiment will your honour wear to-day?

SLY

I am Christophero Sly; call not me 'honour' nor 'lordship:' I **ne'er drank sack in my life**; and if you give me any conserves, give me conserves of beef...

Induction, Scene 2

TRANIO

Sir, I shall not be slack: in sign whereof,
Please ye we may contrive this afternoon,
And **quaff carouses to our mistress' health**,
And do as adversaries do in law,
Strive mightily, but eat and drink as friends.

GRUMIO BIONDELLO

O excellent motion! Fellows, let's be gone.

Act 1, Scene 2

GREMIO

But after many ceremonies done,
He calls for **wine**: 'A health!' quoth he, as if
He had been aboard, **carousing** to his mates
After a storm; **quaff'd off the muscadel**
And threw the sops all in the sexton's face;
Having no other reason
But that his beard grew thin and hungerly
And seem'd to ask him sops as he was **drinking**.

Act 3, Scene 2

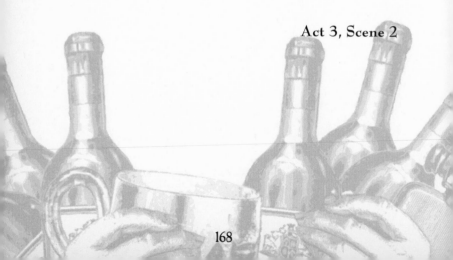

TRANIO

Thou'rt a tall fellow: hold thee that to drink.

Act 4, Scene 4

VINCENTIO

You shall not choose but drink before you go:
think I shall command your welcome here,
And, by all likelihood, some cheer is toward.

Act 5, Scene 1

The Tempest

ANTONIO

We are merely cheated of our lives by drunkards:
This wide-chapp'd rascal – would thou mightst lie drowning
The washing of ten tides!

Act 1, Scene 1

GONZALO

And were the king on't, what would I do?

SEBASTIAN

'Scape being drunk for want of wine.

GONZALO

I' the commonwealth I would by contraries
Execute all things; for no kind of traffic
Would I admit; no name of magistrate;
Letters should not be known; riches, poverty,
And use of service, none; contract, succession,
Bourn, bound of land, tilth, vineyard, none;
No use of metal, corn, or **wine**, or oil;
No occupation; all men idle, all;
And women too, but innocent and pure;
No sovereignty; –

SEBASTIAN

Yet he would be king on't.

Act 2, Scene 1

The Boozy Bard

STEPHANO

He shall taste of my **bottle**: if he have
never **drunk wine** afore will go near to remove his
fit. If I can recover him and keep him tame, I will
not take too much for him; he shall pay for him that
hath him, and that soundly…

STEPHANO

Come on your ways; open your mouth; here is that
which will give language to you, cat: open your
mouth; this will shake your shaking, I can tell you,
and that soundly: you cannot tell who's your friend:
open your chaps again.

TRINCULO

I should know that voice: it should be – but he is
drowned; and these are devils: O defend me!

STEPHANO

Four legs and two voices: a most delicate monster!
His forward voice now is to speak well of his
friend; his backward voice is to utter foul speeches
and to detract. If **all the wine in my bottle** will
recover him, I will help his ague. Come. Amen!
I will pour some in thy other mouth.

CALIBAN

That's a brave god and bears **celestial liquor**.
I will kneel to him.

STEPHANO

How didst thou 'scape? How camest thou hither?
swear by this bottle how thou camest hither. I
escaped upon **a butt of sack** which the sailors
heaved o'erboard, by this bottle; which I made of
the bark of a tree with mine own hands since I was
cast ashore.

CALIBAN

I'll swear upon that bottle to be thy true subject;
for **the liquor is not earthly**.

TRINCULO

By this light, a most perfidious and drunken
monster! when 's god's asleep, he'll rob his bottle.

The Boozy Bard

CALIBAN

A plague upon the tyrant that I serve!
I'll bear him no more sticks, but follow thee,
Thou wondrous man.

TRINCULO

A most ridiculous monster, to make a wonder of a
Poor **drunkard**!

TRINCULO

A howling monster: a **drunken monster**!

Act 2, Scene 2

STEPHANO

My man-monster hath **drown'd his tongue in sack**:
for my part, the sea cannot drown me...

TRINCULO

Why, thou deboshed fish thou,
was there ever man a coward that hath **drunk so much
sack** as I to-day?

CALIBAN

What a pied ninny's this! Thou scurvy patch!
I do beseech thy greatness, give him blows
And take his **bottle** from him: when that's gone
He shall drink nought but brine.

TRINCULO

... Out o' your
wits and bearing too? A pox o' your **bottle**!
this can **sack and drinking** do.

Act 3, Scene 2

The Tempest

PROSPERO

Say again, where didst thou leave these varlets?

ARIEL

I told you, sir, they were **red-hot with drinking**;
So full of valour that they smote the air
For breathing in their faces; beat the ground
For kissing of their feet.

TRINCULO

Ay, but **to lose our bottles** in the pool, –

STEPHANO

There is not only disgrace and dishonour in that,
monster, but an infinite loss.

STEPHANO

Monster, lay-to your fingers: help to bear this
away where my **hogshead of wine** is, or I'll turn you
out of my kingdom: go to, carry this.

Act 4, Scene 1

ALONSO

Is not this Stephano, my **drunken** butler?

SEBASTIAN

He is drunk now: where had he wine?

ALONSO

And Trinculo is reeling ripe: where should they
Find this **grand liquor** that hath gilded 'em?
How camest thou in this pickle?

TRINCULO

I have been in **such a pickle** since I
saw you last that, I fear me, will never out of
my bones: I shall not fear fly-blowing.

CALIBAN

What a thrice-double ass
Was I, to take this drunkard for a god
And worship this dull fool!

Act 5, Scene 1

Twelfth Night

The Boozy Bard

SIR TOBY BELCH

Confine! I'll confine myself no finer than I am:
these clothes are good enough to **drink** in; and so be
these boots too: an they be not, let them hang
themselves in their own straps.

MARIA

That **quaffing and drinking** will undo you: I heard
my lady talk of it yesterday; and of a foolish
knight that you brought in one night here to be her
wooer...
They that add, moreover, he's drunk nightly in your
company.

SIR TOBY BELCH

With drinking healths to my niece: I'll **drink** to
her as long as there is a passage in my throat and
drink in Illyria: he's a coward and a coystrill
that will not **drink to my niece till his brains turn
o' the toe** like a parish-top.

Act 1, Scene 3

OLIVIA

Go to, you're a dry fool; I'll no more of you:
besides, you grow dishonest.

CLOWN

Two faults, madonna, that drink and good counsel
will amend: for **give the dry fool drink, then is
the fool not dry**: bid the dishonest man mend
himself; if he mend, he is no longer dishonest; if
he cannot, let the botcher mend him.

OLIVIA

What's a **drunken man** like, fool?

CLOWN

Like a drowned man, a fool and a mad man: one
draught above heat makes him a fool; the second mads
him; and a third drowns him.

OLIVIA

Go thou and seek the crowner, and let him sit o' my coz; for he's in the **third degree of drink**, he's drowned: go, look after him.

Act 1, Scene 5

SIR ANDREW

I know, to be up late is to be up late.

SIR TOBY BELCH

A false conclusion: I hate it as an unfilled can.
To be up after midnight and to go to bed then, is
early: so that to go to bed after midnight is to go
to bed betimes. Does not our life consist of the
four elements?

SIR ANDREW

Faith, so they say; but I think it rather consists
of eating and drinking.

SIR TOBY BELCH

Thou'rt a scholar; let us therefore eat and drink.
Marian, I say! a stoup of wine!

The Boozy Bard

MALVOLIO

My masters, are you mad? or what are you? Have ye
no wit, manners, nor honesty, but to gabble like
tinkers at this time of night? Do ye make an
alehouse of my lady's house, that ye squeak out your
coziers' catches without any mitigation or remorse
of voice? Is there no respect of place, persons, nor
time in you?

SIR TOBY BELCH

Dost thou think, because thou art
virtuous, there shall be no more cakes and **ale**?

CLOWN

Yes, by Saint Anne, and ginger shall be hot i' the
mouth too.

SIR TOBY BELCH

Thou'rt i' the right. Go, sir, rub your chain with
crumbs. A **stoup of wine**, Maria!

MARIA

The devil a **puritan** that he is, or any thing constantly, but a time-pleaser; an affectioned ass, that cons state without book and utters it by great swarths...

SIR TOBY BELCH

Come, come, I'll go **burn some sack**; 'tis too late to go to bed now: come, knight; come, knight.

Act 2, Scene 3

MALVOLIO

You must **amend your drunkenness**.

Act 2, Scene 5

CLOWN

O, he's drunk, Sir Toby, an hour agone; his eyes were set at eight i' the morning.

SIR TOBY BELCH

Then he's a rogue, and a passy measures panyn: I hate **a drunken rogue**.

Act 5, Scene 1

In 2001, two South African academics claimed that Shakespeare's recreational habits stretched to more than simple alcohol. Several clay pipes were found at the Bard's home (though no one can say for sure if they belonged to him) on which were traced particles of marijuana and cocaine. The scholars point out that Shakespeare – whose drinking buddy Sir Walter Raleigh was responsible for bringing tobacco to British shores – sprinkled his texts with references to 'hemp' and 'weed'. Shakespeare devotees accept that their idol may have smoked such substances for medicinal purposes but deny any possibility that he would have undertaken the activity for pleasure.

The Two
Gentlemen
of Verona

SPEED

'Item: She brews good **ale**.'

LAUNCE

And thereof comes the proverb: 'Blessing of your heart, you brew good ale.'

SPEED

'Item: She will often praise her **liquor**.'

LAUNCE

If her liquor be good, she shall: if she will not, I will; for good things should be praised.

Act 3, Scene 1

Titus Andronicus

TITUS ANDRONICUS

For why my bowels cannot hide her woes,
But **like a drunkard** must I vomit them.
Then give me leave, for losers will have leave
To ease their stomachs with their bitter tongues.

Act 3, Scene 1

Venus and Adonis

The Boozy Bard

Her more than haste is mated with delays,
Like the proceedings of **a drunken brain**,
Full of respects, yet nought at all respecting,
In hand with all things, nought at all effecting.

Lines 909–912

The Winter's Tale

AUTOLYCUS

For **a quart of ale** is a dish for a king.

Act 4, Scene 3

CLOWN

If it be ne'er so false, a true gentleman may swear
it in the behalf of his friend: and I'll swear to
the prince thou art a tall fellow of thy hands and
that **thou wilt not be drunk**; but I know thou art no
tall fellow of thy hands and that **thou wilt be
drunk**: but I'll swear it, and I would thou wouldst
be a tall fellow of thy hands.

Act 5, Scene 2

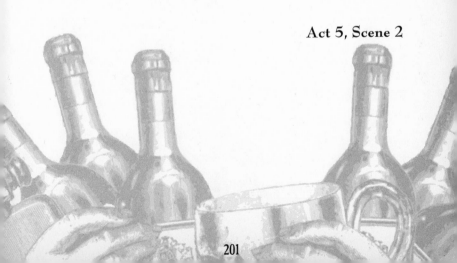

Brit Wit

The perfect riposte for every social occasion

Edited by
Susie Jones

Brit Wit

The perfect riposte for every social occasion

Susie Jones

Hb

'*It is a good thing for an uneducated man to read books of quotations.*'
                                                    Sir Winston Churchill

Ever been at a loss for words? Ever wished you had the perfect put down or wry remark for every socially awkward situation? The great, the good, the intellectual and the downright insulting can all be found in *Brit Wit*.

Densely overpopulated with wonderful one-liners from such formidable figures as Churchill and Shakespeare, to the more recent luminaries of British stage, screen and society, *Brit Wit* celebrates all that makes Britain brilliant.

We are amused.

MORE Brit Wit

The perfect riposte for every social occasion

More Brit Wit

The perfect riposte for every social occasion

Hb

Need a wry remark for that all-important speech, or a pithy put down for that caustic colleague? This follow-up to the bestselling *Brit Wit* will elevate your verbal repartee to a whole new level.

Learn more about the art of the epigram from brilliant Old Blighty's wittiest and wisest, from Jane Austen to Billy Connolly and Geoffrey Chaucer to Tracey Emin.

What the Victorians *Didn't* Do for Us

A collection of their useless advice

Beatrice Hemsworth

What the Victorians *didn't* do for us

A collection of their useless advice

Beatrice Hemsworth

Hb

Did you know that washing your teeth with charcoal was once believed to make them whiter? That ladies were encouraged to drink vinegar to appear pale and delicate?

The Victorians may have given us the Industrial Revolution and advances in medicine and science, but they also relied on child labour and extolled the benefits of opium. From the strange to the downright unsavoury, learn what the Victorians *didn't* do for us.